PERSUASION'S PRICE

A play
by Sam Grant

© Sam Grant 2021

The rights of Sam Grant to be identified as the author of this work have been asserted by him in accordance with the Copyright, Designs and Patents Act of 1988.

All rights reserved; no part of this publication may be reproduced, stored in a retrieval system, or transmitted in any form or by any means, electronic, mechanical, photocopying, recording or otherwise without the prior written consent of the publisher or a licence permitting copying in the UK issued by the Copyright Licensing Agency Ltd. www.cla.co.uk

ISBN 978-1-78222-870-7

Book design, layout and production management by Into Print
www.intoprint.net

01604 832149

Introductory music:

Prokofiev Symphony No. 1 "Classical"

Third Movement Non troppo allegro (1.27)

Jason Whatley, narrator enters stage right.

"-There you are *(notices audience)* you know, the powers that be; the hirers and firers. It was their suggestion, that an introduction might paint a picture, start the ball rolling - get you lot on board, so to speak. Needed to be an outsider. Someone who'd pass as an ordinary, Joe, though, and they said, you've got an ordinary look about you – no flattery there!"

"Jason, it's an acting promotion, from extra - soldier at Waterloo, for you." That, being my last job. I'd get to say something, this time, you see. Yep, proper actor fashion, not just march about, in soldier garb, with a musket …Funnily, enough, I was down at the Trellis and Vine at the time. Yes …. that's, where the production finished, but the beginning for this story, was Linton farm. *Pauses, for reflection.*

Pleasant enough couple – that's John and Dot and, then, their daughter, Vicky. A beauty who was never going to settle down, for life on Linton farm. That's not as farmer's wife! Once she'd been to Uni - big wide world was going to be more exciting. See, I was at work on their boiler, previous to being on my way, to the Trellis. Yes, it all started at Linton Farm, but back pre – corona virus - August, 2019, I guess. Seems like a look at another world, if you ask me. I'll let you see for yourselves though. *Exit stage left.*

Cast in order of appearance
Act One – Linton Farm

Jason Whatley: Domestic boiler, plumbing engineer. **Narrator.**

John Leadley: farmer, at Linton Farm. Setting in the south west of England

Dorothy (Dot): Leadley: wife, to John Leadley

Luke: young farm labourer. Seventeen to eighteen years of age.

Taras Kedrov: Russian mafia/gangster. Marine engineering background, with store in Brodham

Izabella: partner to Taras. Has a cosmetics and fashion business, online. Friends with Russian president.

Anton Carter (Kedrov) Taras's son, by marriage to Alsa. Taras and Alsa, divorced when Anton was a child. Anton, subsequently grew up and was educated in England, and seeks to steer his father toward running a legitimate company, away from nefarious drug and gold smuggling. Respected owner of Investment Fund – Zircon Distribution. Golf club member, polo player and church sidesman.

Vicky (Victoria): Dot and John's daughter, who has returned to their farm from University, after completing her degree.

Carin: Personal Assistant to Anton. *(Name first mentioned in mobile phone call)*

Carol: hospitality employee – Trellis and Vine *(name, first mentioned on phone with Vicky)*

Danny*:* Postman: first, on stage appearance at Linton Farm.

Act Two – Meeting Room: Trellis and Vine

Oleg: Russian associate to Taras and Izabella. Oleg, speaks English more fluently than Yakov.

Yakov: Second Russian associate.

Act Three – Double Bedroom – Trellis and Vine. Public House with guest rooms.

Carin: Personal Assistant to Anton Carter (Kedrov) Secures position as chauffeur, after retirement of Henry at head office – Zircon Distribution

Act Four – Heron Tower – Penthouse suite number 10

Tom Draycot: Junior Transport Minister

Reynolds: security chief – special services.

Jane Albright: Secretary – civil servant.

Two Civil Servants – attendant on Jane Albright

Two Security guards – stand by window – either side

Alison: administrator grade.

Two lap top desk set up civil servants – with Alison

_____ interval_____

Introductory music to second half:

Beethoven: Turkish March from The Ruins of Athens Incidental music, Op.113 (1.46) Royal Philharmonic Orchestra conducted by Sir Thomas Beecham ch 1958

Act Five : Izabella's Office.

Eva: Supervisor for Izabella's online, listings. Brodham office.

Act Six: Carin informed about motor home

Veronica: Carin's boss working in intelligence services

Act Seven: Scene One

Curtain close - followed by swift re-opening.

Act Seven: Scene Two

George: Publican – owner, Trellis and Vine – Married to Suzi – Asian wife.

Suzi: George's Asian Wife. Young woman - oriental accented, speech (calls from backstage)

Act Eight: (interchange of Post Office to Bar) Act Four: (design interchange for Trellis and Vine bar to post office facility)

Annette: Sub postmistress at Frampton post office. Young woman. Late twenties, early thirties. (construct, of stage "Lay by," (**Act 5**) **assembled,** mid front stage**,** of Trellis and Vine for ease of dispersal into finale - Act 10, staged in Trellis and Vine bar area)

Act Nine:

Police one: Traffic policeman – in uniform.

Police two: Police two: Traffic policeman – in uniform.

Motor Home Occupant one: male, foreign national denoted by broken English accent.

Motor Home Occupant Two: Female.

Act Ten: Bar. Trellis and Vine.

George Baxter: Landlord: Trellis and Vine.

PERSUASION'S PRICE

A play
by Sam Grant

Act One: Scene One

Stage setting: Linton Farm. Cooking range. Mantle piece with photos of farm. Window looks out on to farmyard. Stairway near to stage right – leads down to sitting area – kitchen diner effect – kitchen table set stage left – cooker behind.

Prize rosetted bull photo - farmer in white coat hat on shelf above cooker. Kitchen diner set up - with breakfast table by cooker with green enamelled coffee jug, mugs and dark tin biscuit barrel – not glass, ready for Danny's arrival, on table.

- Two arm chairs; settee and coffee table stage right – Fourth wall – audience.
- Luke's breakfast items cereal packet – plate, mug, jug, sugar bowl on kitchen table.

On stage – as curtain rises. John Leadley, Dot Leadley, Luke. John, is sat in best arm chair, angled marginally toward audience. Luke's sat at kitchen table – faces, audience - on his smart phone. Dot is folding cloths to hang on cooker rail **(curtain rise)** and calls to Luke, before completion of curtain opening. Dot is folding cloths to hang on cooker rail and calls to Luke, before completion of curtain opening.

Dot: 'Luke.' *She calls out. He appears, not to hear – busy on phone. Dot, wears a skirt with apron – knitted top. Slippers. Luke – hi vis trousers, tee shirt and open hooded type top and is in stockinged feet*

Dot: - 'Luke! I'm speaking to you!'

Luke: 'With you, with you Mrs Led,' *on game – does, momentarily look across but is still on game. John Leadley, has papers on the coffee table, which he's comparing against a lap top. Dot, removes casserole from oven, lifts lid, looks and sniffs. Replaces lid, and calls once more to Luke.*

Dot: 'You'll be wanting something this evening?'

Luke: 'If that's poss, Mrs Led.'

Dot: A casserole, Luke. It'll be in a bowl, in the fridge. Needs four minutes, in the microwave and help yourself to a cornetto from the freezer.' *John doesn't look up from his lap top in his response.*

John: 'Ragged Duck will be closing down, without you there for a meal, Luke.

Luke: 'Ragged Duck's no match for Mrs Leds casserole.' *Luke takes a drink from his mug and puts phone in pocket.*

Dot: 'I'm pleased to hear that, Luke.' *Sound of motor – Range Rover from outside window. Luke puts down phone. Goes to window. Stage left.*

Luke: 'That's some motor, out there Mr Led. Don't see many like them, in these parts. What'll he be wanting?'

Dot: 'Never you mind. It's gone eleven. You should be out in them fields. Hadn't you?' *John shuts down his lap top and gets up, whilst saying,*

John: 'I'll see to them. Be with you, in a while, Luke.' *turns towards Luke.* You can take the tractor up to the field. Fill her up before you go, mind.' *Luke goes to door stage left – in stockinged feet. Puts on wellington boots – turned down. Pick's cap and coat from hooks at side of door. Leaves by door, near to kitchen. Stage left. Almost immediately, voices can be heard outside. Car door slams, footstep approach. Knocker taps five times – two, two, one.*

Izabella and Taras voices – heard from off stage. To enter stage right. Followed by Anton, who has a lap top, in case, and a wallet with documents.

Izabella: 'It is so peaceful. I like this okay, Taras.

Taras: I said you would, cherie.

John: 'They'll be the new tenants from Turnbull and Atkins, about the barns.' *Dot removes apron and tidies hair before wall mirror. John walks across, buttoning waistcoat, making himself presentable - opens latched door. Taras speaks.*

Taras: Good morning. We are not inconvenient? (*announces himself*) - Taras Kedrov, my partner Izabella and son Anton. *Dress:* **Taras:** *City suit – pin stripe. White shirt. Brogue/brown shoes. Bright tie.*

John: Expecting you – yes, yes, come in, won't you. Turnbull and Atkins, have been in contact. *Greeting smile. Taras and Anton enter farm house. Taras, makes move to shake hands. John shakes Taras's and Anton's hand. Dot walks over and smiles toward Izabella, as she enters.*

Anton: Yes, we have all the details My father, would like a look around. I have the paper work. Like to have a look first, but from online photos the barns look ideal.

John: Good, good.

Taras: Anton, my son deals with the admin side of the business.

Dot: You mustn't mind us we breakfast late with an early start. There's tea in the pot if you would- *Taras, smiles toward Dot – on interruption.*

Taras: -That would be most welcome, wouldn't it cherie? *(looks toward Izabella, to include) Izabella, not overly interested, nods and makes hand gesture.*

Dress: *Anton*, *in jeans, blazer, and collared, casual top shirt – no tie and smart suitably matched navy/black trainers – not white.*
Izabella. *In black leggings, mini length skirt, necklace – pebble - like, red, brown, blue and green. Gemstone ring, on right but not left -hand fingers. Gold bracelet on right wrist – wave of arm to display – when speaking in early scene, but not later. Tasselled hand bag. Moderate or high heels. Not trainers!*

Izabella: It is good to escape from the town. You've horses I, see?' *By this time, they are into the room and Dot is ushering them across to the settee area.*

Dot: A mare and a foal. *Taras just ahead of John, admires the photo of a bull with rosette, in silver frame on mantlepiece.*

Taras: A magnificent beast. May I? *He reaches out, as if to pick up the photo frame. First smiling toward John.*

John: By all means. That was July 2018. Best in show. Taras holds the photo up to get a better look.

Taras: Yes, I can see why; beautiful beast.

Izabella, sits herself on middle of settee, forces Anton to sit near to her. John, directs Taras with hand movement to arm chair, opposite him. Two armchairs, each side of mantlepiece. Stage back wall – Taras sits, stage left, with chair angled toward three-seater settee for seating Anton and Izabella. Angled for audience view; opposite two cushioned kitchen type chairs.

Izabella looks across to the window.

Izabella: For me it is the horse that is most beautiful.

Taras: They are both beautiful animals, Cherie.

Dot: Izabella how do you take tea? Sugar and milk?

Izabella: Half tea and half hot water. No sugar or milk. *John and Taras make conversation across the fire hearth – (John to Taras – you found us alright etc… No trouble we saw the sign to Linton Farm on the roadside.) Anton responds to the tea question.*

Anton: Thank you Mrs Leadley. Tea with splash of milk will be fine, for father and me.

Taras: Mr Leadley we have shipments of machinery. Mainly marine valves and fittings to do with my business, John, may I call you John?

Anton sets up laptop from case and papers to place on coffee table. Izabella is texting on phone.

John: Fine by me. *Opens and clasps hands in acknowledgement.*

Will this be by lorry? The road leading to the farm isn't up to much.

Anton: No problem We'd be prepared to rebuild your road, Mr Leadley, to meet requirements. That's if you have no objection?

John: None, at all – I can assure you of that!

Taras: I've spoken with David Turnbull and you may be accepting of three months advance payment? *John lightens up still further with the rent response.*

John: No objection on both counts. Some machineries to go out of a barn, and they'll be ready for you. You'll need racking, I guess? Getting ahead of myself, but…

Anton: Yes, that's okay, we've a Brodham firm lined up, If that's okay, with you. You probably know Barnaby and Banks. *Anton inspects a paper – reading glasses on - next to the lap top he's set up on the coffee table. Dot arrives with a tray with three porcelain flowered mugs of tea. Anton removes lap top/ papers.*

Izabella: Mrs Leadley you are my rescuer from talk about machinery, lorries and roads. *Dot places the tray down on the table.*

Dot: One nearest, is yours Izabella. Perhaps you'd like to see Cleopatra with her foal in a moment?

Izabella: That would be most agreeable. *Taras gets up to take his mug of tea.*

Taras: There cherie, *(speaks to Izabella, before sitting back down)* I knew that you would find our visit interesting. *smiles, for approval from Izabella.*

Izabella: *(shrugs)* I have no problem with visit. It's just talk, about business and how to get crates from A to B, I do not care for. We still need Taras, to find somewhere for a meal. *They sip tea, in process of ongoing conversation.*

Anton: The Trellis and Vine does meals, apparently, that's nearby.

John: Yes. We've been there on occasion. Nothing fancy. They've a menu and booking app. You can order online before you get there, I believe.

Anton: I'll get it up, Trellis and Vine. – *(He gets it up online and shows Izabella.)* There *follows discussion, with Izabella nods head in agreement – John and Taras continue chat.)*

John: When do you need to move your machinery crates in?

Taras: It'll be next month. I have managers to organize this. If that is alright. Do you John have by any a chance a fork lifter?

John: Can manage that. Probably supply a driver, if you're agreeable to a daily charge of say, sixty pounds, plus labour.

Taras: Not a problem that would be excellent. *John smiles at Dot – things are coming up roses. Izabella puts porcelain mug down.*

Izabella: Now we have booked table for lunch: can I see the horses?'

Dot: Of course, if everyone's ready. *Taras gets up together with John. (Vicky, descends stairs, brushing hair – stops to place hair brush on stairs before going to kitchen area.*

Dot: Vicky, we're going to see Cleopatra – *smiles, acknowledgements. Taras turns to Izabella.*

Taras: Yes, cherie I can have a look at the barns and you can see the horses. If that's agreeable? *He turns toward John. Izabella seductively straightens leg to apparently adjust leggings and get Anton's attention, but he's working on his iPad – fails.*

Anton: I'll stay here father, I've some work to catch up on.

Dot: Of course. *Dot smiles at Vicky, who is making instant coffee.*

John: we can reach the barns through the yard. I'll lead the way.

_____Curtain_____

Act One: Scene Two

Return curtain rise - with Anton – Laptop is open on table. Case next to chair. Visible to audience. Now holds iPhone and is chatting with Carin.

Anton: Carin, Carin. Hi, where are you? *Pause for answer.* How long? - Probably within the hour. *Pause.* Yep. It's looking like a long day. Can you book us in. *Slight pause.* Get back to me Carin. Bye. *Puts down phone. Returns to lap top – compares contract on table with screen details. Vicky, in midst of making coffee – instant from jar – no milk. kettle boils rapidly – pre- boiled. Turns across from kitchen area.*

Vicky: Are you Russian? You don't sound foreign. *Anton, Looks, up from work on laptop, in politeness - toward Vicky – and yes! She's, an attractive young woman.*

Anton: I was five when I came to England with my mother.

Vicky: Don't let me disturb you. I only came down for a coffee. *Vicky looks toward where Anton's pad and work is.*

Anton: No. no you're not. I've about finished. *Shuts down lap top – closes lid.* And, you work the farm with your mother and father?

Vicky: Not really. I'm back from university, for the summer. Help out, but farm families do. And you?

Anton: I'm assisting my father. *Vicky moves, toward, her father's chair, coffee in hand.*

Vicky: Right. *– times this, with sitting down.*

Anton: Izabella -

Vicky: "Izabella." That's a name that sounds as if it might be Russian.

Anton: Yes, that comes across.

Vicky: Is she your sister? I don't want to sound nosy.

Anton: no, no, it's alright – Izabella's father's partner.

Vicky: Sounds a bit complicated.

Anton: Not, really. Father and mother divorced on arrival, in England. Izabella's, quite new on the scene. I'm really, only here to get father settled – just booked in at the Trellis and Vine. Is it?

Vicky: It's good - Got to say that, really – work there. Holiday work. Your wife… Carin? Is she new to the area?

Anton: Carin? Oh, no, no - Carin's my Personal Assistant. *Vicky gives expression of - Oh my – out of view of Anton. Not that Carin's, not his wife – but that he has a PA!*

Dot and Izabella return. Enter stage right.

Izabella: That's lovely. *(Remarks to Dot)* A beautiful horse, but she's not staying, here? *Interjection from Vicky*

Vicky: - No. Cleopatra has to return to her owner next week. Doesn't she mother?

Dot: It was what we agreed, but Annetta has asked me if you would like to exercise Cleo once or twice a week. *Izabella interrupts.*

Izabella: Annetta? Not Annetta Hastings, at West Frampton Post Office.

Dot: Annetta Hastings, yes.

Vicky: And yes, you know I would, mother. *Vicky, gets up goes with phone to sit at kitchen table.*

Izabella: But then, I would so like, to ride again. *Sits back next to Anton.* We just need another horse and we could go riding together, Anton. *When Izabella turns back to speak - Anton, unseen by Izabella, he nods head from side to side – negative response.*

I must speak with Annetta. We attend Latin American dance lessons, you know.

Dot: You and Taras?

Izabella: No – no, no! *John and Taras have entered stage right – in hushed tone on Taras' approach-* Taras he has what is it you say? Two left feet.

Loud interjection from Taras.

Taras – that is very agreeable for us, John. *Taras notices Izabella*

Taras: Ah, you are back as well cherie. Everything's tickety boo. Is that not an English way of compliment? *Does not sit down. Anton is shutting down lap top – gathering papers from desk*

John: Sort of. - *John gives puzzled look.*

Taras: There'll still be, paperwork to complete, yes? *Includes Anton* Perhaps, Anton can visit again to complete. We have few weeks to organize transport. Two of my managers to organize unloading, as we talked about, if that is okay, John?

John: Turnbull and Atkins will handle the contract side of things. *Izabella stands up. Impatient to be going.*

Anton: No worries, Mr Leadley, they've been very helpful. *Izabella turns to Dot*

Izabella: So good to offer us tea and to see Cleopatra. I am going to ask Annetta, she may allow me to ride Cleopatra, Taras?

Taras: This horse belongs to your friend Annetta, that's good cherie. *Pause.* Ah, yes you are all welcome to visit my store - in town.

Izabella: They'll not be interested to see marine valves, Taras. *Anton's phone rings*

But perhaps Dorothy, you might be interested to see my cosmetic and fashion range.

Dot: *(smiles)* -Thank you Izabella.

Anton: *(on phone)* Hi Carin. *Pause.* Yes, that's fine. A double for me, will do okay, if that's all they have. Catch up with you there, later. *Pause* Okay, Carin.

Taras: John, it's all settled, for me. *Calls across to Anton.* Anton, you can call back to finalize plans with John, later, yes?

Anton: That's the plan father. *Anton is packing his papers/ laptop away.* A table for twelve is booked at the Trellis and Vine. *Taras turns to John – holds out hand, which John shakes, a bit bemused, by seemingly overly courteous behaviour – what's it all about?*

Taras: You're so kind to give your time to show me around John.

John: Perfectly alright. Looks across to Anton. We'll expect a call then?

Anton: Yes, within a fortnight at the latest. *Izabella's phone rings*

Izabella: One moment. I am so sorry. *Answers.*

Yes, Oleg what is it. *Pause. Removes phone from ear.* Taras, it is Oleg. They're back from the N E C. *Taras reaches out – to take phone, but is for – stalled.*

Taras: Let me speak with them, cherie.

Izabella: No Taras, it is me they want to speak with.

Taras: Taras: Please, tell them cherie, I'll expect them. At the Trellis and Vine, no later than two, this afternoon.

Izabella: (on phone) – yes, yes later we will speak. Be at the Trellis and Vine near Brodham, for two o'clock, okay. Bye.

Taras: *Turns to John.* My apologies, John, I'm exhibiting at the NEC and two staff are returned. Thank you so much for tea, again Mrs Leadley and to meet you all. *Vicky smiles from where she's sat. Dot is clearing Luke's breakfast things from kitchen table*

Taras: So good to meet you. Anton will be in touch. *John goes to door and shows them out. John meanwhile has smart phone in hand. Taps/scans in walk across – aside*

John: Yields are down, again.

Dot: Count your chickens, John, – the barns are near let! *Share of confidence, with Vicky, sat at kitchen table. Audience facing. Table lengthwise to stage front. Danny's place is at end of table stage left.*

Dot: Look at the time. We've an appointment with the accountant. Places tray on kitchen drainer. *Walks across to fetch anorak, hung up. Back wall stage left near door*

John: Yep, I'm ready. *On phone, but goes to fetch hat from behind door, stage right.*

Dot: You can see to Danny, Vicky; he'll be next.. Coffees on the hob. *Talks, as she walks and puts on anorak, to meet with John to exit stage right.*

Vicky: What's the fuss? He's just the postman.

Dot: And yes, Vicky - that letter *(points to mantlepiece)* for M&S, on the mantlepiece is to go – make sure it does! *John exits stage right. Vicky taps phone, to contact Carol.*

Vicky: - Hi, Carol. Are you on your, own? Expect visitors. *Pause.*

A Russian family, are on their way. *Pause.* Yes, I've not forgotten I'm on at two.

Curtain

Act One - Scene Three

"Twelve second interval before curtain rise." Sound of post van parking up – Stage right.

Vicky is sat at table on smart phone. Legs on chair pulled out.

Red mug, biscuit barrel/ tin/ Horse and Hound/ Farmer's Weekly *magazine, on kitchen table, near to where Danny will sit. Three taps on door and then he walks in newspaper under arm – audience facing – rifling letters – places, for example, smaller letters to front of largest one*

(Largest envelope (A4) addressed to Mr Taras Kedrov, Managing Director, Kedrov Marine Valves & Machinery, Linton Farm, East Frampton, Nr to Brodham BQ10 B5X, plus three smaller ones – (can drop a letter and pick up, if time allows, whilst sort walk across stage front to kitchen table - offset – (practised, letter throw of letters, newspaper to table - interrupted by Vicky's 'questioning.'

Danny entering, stage right, as curtain opens, with Vicky speaking.

Vicky: You didn't expect him to, did you? *Notices Danny, lowers phone - 'Anything for me Danny? - Hold on Carol. Danny makes to look through letters, nods head side to side and enquires -*

Danny: Is it your birthday then? *Practised throw - letters and newspaper on table, from Danny, before he walks across to hob.*

Vicky: No, but there might be a letter. *Danny, removes kitchen gloves from cooker rail to pick enamel jug off hob. Walks with jug to kitchen table - pours coffee in to mug (laughter from Vicky on phone, in chat with Carol) – Danny, places, jug on table, near to mug. – returns gloves to rail, before sitting down.*

Vicky: Really! you don't mean that! – no! *More shared merriment, before quietening down*

Danny, meanwhile, sits down at table removes lid of held biscuit barrel, looks inside, to select biscuit. Takes out one, and bites small piece. Opens edition of Horse and Hound/Farmer's weekly. Smooths down middle of magazine.

Vicky: Do you want me to? I can ask him, he's here now. *Vicky draws arm, away from phone. Danny is sipping coffee with opened Farmers weekly*

Vicky: Carol, wants to know if she can re- join the Wimbledon group? *Returns to phone* I'll go with you, Carol. *Danny's flicks through Farmer's Weekly, before replying.*

Danny: Maybe.

Vicky: Carol, he said, maybe.

Danny: *Opens flat, edition of Horse and Hound/ Farmer's Weekly- looks at page.*

Danny: Okay, then.

Vicky: You can, now, apparently.

Danny: *Without looking up from Farmer's Weekly.* Tell Carol; that I miss her, at the net, to smash Alex's return - from back of court. *Takes sip of coffee.*

Vicky: He misses you at the net. Danny, misses you at the net, smashing Alex's back of court return. *Pause.* He said that to you? What did you say? *Pause* That's what I do, Carol; threaten that I'll tell Suzi. Runs around after George, but that's only for front of house. George, dare not put a foot out of place. Yep, always threaten to tell Suzi. *(sound of Land Rover returning)* - have to go, parents are back - See you, bye.

Danny: *Places part biscuit, in mouth and swigs down remainder of coffee.* I've got a be going. *Danny gets up, walks over to door, stage right. Smiles, holds door open for Dot, who enters, with environmentally friendly shopping bag in right hand.*

Dot: *Calls over to Vicky.* Your father wants you help muck out Cleo's stable, before you go riding when you're back from the Trellis. Hold on Danny. *Calls out; Dot smiles, more subdued. Points toward letter on mantlepiece.* It's just as well I'm back. *Walks across and picks letter off mantlepiece.*

Can you take that for me please Danny? *Walks back to hand letter to Danny.*

Danny: Of course, Mrs Leadley. *(takes letter)* Thanks for the coffee and biscuits.

Dot: You know you're welcome Danny. *Vicky mimics her mother. Danny opens door – goes out, reappears and calls back.*

Danny: Mrs Leadley, you've got a visitor. *and exits*

Dot: It'd better be that Jason Whatley or I'll want to know why? *Jason Whatley (narrator) enters with tool bag and copper piping.*

Jason: Got held up in traffic. Soon get that boiler back in action, Mrs Leadley.

_____Curtain_____

Act Two: – Persuasion's Price.

Meeting Room at Trellis and Vine.

Low-level – coffee table. Door entrance – stage left – set away from mid stage toward stage right. Fireplace/mantlepiece centre, back stage. Yakov, sat in easy chair with iPad – sideways to audience - playing game on iPad. Main conference table has beige/brown tablecloth; cream china vase with five red roses; table length wise – end on to audience. Spare chairs stacked back stage right and left. Table head chair – facing audience for Taras. Two chairs either side. Anton will be on his right; Izabella on left. Table seating plan: Taras – table head. Anton on right. Yakov next to Anton Izabella, on left. Oleg next to Izabella.

> *Oleg enters briskly - stage left– phone in hand. Oleg next to Izabella; Yakov next to Anton, who holds a document folder, which is placed on the table, as he sits down*

Oleg: Yakov it is the girl. *Points at screen whilst walking/talking.* That girl in the bar. *Yakov is sat on chair with iPad. Leg stretched across adjacent chair at table.*

Yakov: Are you sure. And why does it matter, Oleg? *Shows phone with photo to Yakov, before he sits down chair stage right to Yakov.*

Oleg: Izabella, will know, if it is. Izabella, will want to know more.

Yakov: Why, my friend?'

Oleg: This: is a desirable person site. Others, may be interested to have ownership. And they will pay well.

Yakov: So, it's Slave trafficking - *waves hand dismissively* - Ahmed from NEC does not drink. With Taras - white slave trade - pfffffffff - Anton? Anton, he'd go ballistic, you know that, Oleg.

Oleg: Okay, but when Izabella's on her own. I think she can be persuaded. We need to say that it is something of interest, from the N E C, no more than that Yakov. *Taras's voice, off stage."*

Taras: I will visit English pubs more often, with customers. It will be good for business."

Yakov: They're coming. Get that photo off the screen. *Both are sat on settee, but get up to move toward table, which has beige/brown tablecloth; cream china vase with five red roses. Taras strides,* stage left, *followed by Anton, both holding a red document folder. Izabella, whose off stage, turns to talk to Vicky, who's outside.*

Izabella: That's right, Vicky. Two gin and tonic with lemon and half pint of Brodham

Taras: Returned from a successful show you two, no? *Pulls back chair, together with others, to sit around table. Whilst settling Oleg responds: -*

Oleg: We successfully switched a valve with the Chinese. And Taras, *(smiles),* you have a Swedish company that wants to buy your mega star underwater valve.

Anton: That's good, father, you're establishing yourself, as a legitimate engineering specialist, *Taras shrugs/ chooses to ignore remark. Looks inside folder.*

Izabella: And the hotel. It has problems? We understand? Has it not?

Anton: Problems with what?'

Oleg: You don't have a drink Izabella. I can order one for you?

Izabella: They're ordered already. Don't avoid my question. Oleg.

Yakov: It was so, unfortunate, Izabella. A previous manager was heard to talk about a guest, a senior agent, in the bar - loose tongued, you know. *Knock on door. Door opens. Stage left. Vicky enters with tray of drinks. - Oleg to Yakov – understood look.*

Izabella: A surprise, for us. Thank you, Vicky – yes on the table, that will be fine.

Vicky: Oh George, I mean Mr Baxter, said to tell you, (looks at Anton,) that Carin Hanson has arrived.

Anton: Thank you. Could you tell her Vicky that I've booked in for the night and perhaps she'd like to have the cases put in the rooms.

Vicky: Yes sir, *(smiles, somewhat superciliously)* will there be anything else?

Izabella: No, Vicky, that is all. *Vicky leaves and closes door.*

Taras: And Yakov? –

Yakov: Oleg. He will best explain.

Oleg: Okay, I'll explain the situation, Taras. Well, it is that he became high risk, to us, you see, Taras, and to our valued guests, of course. It was unfortunate, the hotel lift, out of action, not to use sign, was removed mid – afternoon. Next day, he was helped, to walk into the lift's empty space, on his way, you understand, from office to ground floor. You could say he arrived more quickly, than might be expected. Reception, reported a scream, followed by a thud. An ambulance was called, but unfortunately…

Izabella: Has it been recorded as an accident? I mean – are we in any way liable?

Oleg: But yes. I mean it's recorded, but not in a bad way for the hotel. The sign was in place for everyone else in the hotel. You understand?

Taras: So, what does that mean?

Oleg: It's okay, Taras, it's sorted. We made sure a good amount of barbiturate was in the body, before it was taken away. Cause of death was later recorded as misadventure. I was able to talk with the coroner, Taras. It was good, but bad, if you understand.

Anton: What do you mean by that?

Oleg: He'd recently parted from his wife. A depressed man, you see. So sad, we both agreed. It was terrible that his stepping into the lift shaft, pointed to suicide, whilst his balance of mind, was disturbed.

Taras: The new manager? He has been well vetted?

Oleg: But of course. He's previously from the hospitality department, at the civil service. And it is very good, he has signed their official secrets act. He will keep secret whatever he hears and we've been able to have regular customers build debt, but of course establish, they have funds to cover them. Additional service is available from our young women, who work the casino. They're paid twenty per cent, out of the hotel payment, for services. But it can be a struggle to pay bills, even so.

Taras: Yakov, more importantly, you have information about a corridor through Europe for arms and drugs, to incite revolution and disorder, in the outer areas of Italy. A plan to extricate gold from Vatican City Vaults and Rome to finance a revolutionary force. And Now we have facilities to store ingots.

Yakov: Yes, that is good Taras.

Anton: Father, *(despairing tone)* you said that you were going legal, now the valve engineering firm, is near to set up. This sounds like craziness!

Taras: Just one last taste of adventure, Anton, before I'm part, of English business furniture. Safe and solid. Gold, will be held in the barns for a limited time, in boxes, marked up as engineering parts. No one will know otherwise. It's a business contract, that will pay well.

Izabella: It is very okay. I'll have my online cosmetics and fashion business and Taras will be back to his first love for engineering, won't you?

Taras: You see Anton, it needs to be gradual. We know these people in Italy. It will be good. Now let's turn to the Buy to Let portfolio. How many are there now Anton? *Anton opens folder on table. Holds up paper. Reads from: -*

Anton: Five, and a new hotel is in negotiation. Suggest that this property group together with hotels is made into a limited company. If you are in agreement father, it will have a British name.

Izabella: Have you any ideas Anton?'

Anton: How about Blackthorn. An English sounding name.

Taras: Yes, why not. You two, *(points to Oleg and Yakov),* Anton will look at the hotel's books in a month's time. These accounts need to go to Joules, the accountant. You'll need to cover gambling and escort services, as alternative expenditure from guests.

Yakov: we already do this Taras, West end theatres give us tickets for guests, at very reasonable prices. You know theatres like to make it appear that seats are reserved, to impress critics. That's when they are not there, to watch, but need to make - up a report. It's helpful to have record ticket sales, especially when no one goes to watch, they say. Also, we've added health spa charges, for men and women. Guests, can be booked in to play golf.

Anton: Didn't know you were so keen on theatre, Yakov? *(bit, on sarcastic side)*

Yakov: Not me, Anton. It is Tamara. She likes to be seen going to the theatre. And I have to show interest, you know. *Looks toward Taras, for sympathetic understanding.*

Izabella: That's all okay, but did you make any contacts that I might have interest for?

Oleg: Maybe, Izabella, Maybe. *Smiles knowingly, but not obviously, toward Yakov*

Taras: If it's in the cosmetics or fashion line…

Oleg: Possibly.

Taras: In that case, this meeting can end. Anton. I'm going for a cider. You see I have transformed, to a very local person.

Anton: I'll join you. *Anton, closes folder. Gets up, followed by Taras. They leave. Exit stage left.*

Izabella, moves chair back, imperiously and gets up, to sit expansively, on settee, where Yakov sat, earlier in scene.

Izabella: Well, what have you that might interest me then? *Removes, gold cigarette case and lighter from handbag – opens cigarette case, selects cigarette, shuts case. Taps cigarette on cigarette case, to command attention.*

Izabella: Well, what have you, that might be of interest?

Izabella: Well? *Light's cigarette.*

Oleg: It is not in the cosmetics or fashion business. You perhaps might not be that interested. *(Oleg, fishing, to get Izabella's attention)*

Yakov: Something that Ahmed showed us. We didn't take that much interest, because you are no longer in the business Izabella.

Izabella: And what is that?

Yakov: Show Izabella the photos. *Oleg brings photos up on iPad. Starts flicking through photos. Gets up and goes to sit next to Izabella.*

Izabella: They're photos of young women and men. What is this an online dating site.?

Oleg: Sort of it is, Izabella. But do you see anyone you know?

Izabella: That one. It is the girl from the farm. She is waitress, yes? She is with a horse, I have seen. So? Perhaps, she looks for a boyfriend? What is strange about that?

Yakov: It's not like that, Izabella.

Oleg: These are photos of persons, that have appeal for wealthy clients, who, are prepared, to pay to have these people, how shall I say? To take from the country. Their passports are confiscated. Some go believing, that they have good employment and do not become missing persons, for much later.

Izabella: And this girl?

Oleg: Ahmed. You know, Ahmed, at the NEC, he said Prince Azid, wants this girl.

Izabella: And so?

Oleg: He's offered to buy the horse, ridden by the girl. He was at the same university.

Izabella: And the girl?

Yakov: Yes.

Izabella: And of course, the horse, it will be most expensive to transport. More expensive than the girl.

Oleg: Maybe, but a good cover. There's half a million available, in instalments, for an intermediary, to assist, with full payment, when she arrives in Saudi Arabia. The captors need to be informed of her movements.

Izabella: That is a persuasive amount. I cannot disagree.

Yakov: We said, didn't we Oleg, *(Oleg nods head in affirmation)* - this arrangement might be of interest, to you Izabella.

Izabella: Who are the captors?

Yakov: Two persons, from China are to assist Prince Azid. Their motor home will be near to place, where the horse is stabled, to take her away, when time is right. You're a horse woman Izabella and the young woman, also.

Izabella: I am not directly involved in the kidnap?

Yakov: Of course not. You are just facilitator. To make it so, trusts both you and them, you understand? Once successfully aboard the motor home, you'll receive a tranche of two hundred and fifty thousand pounds. The other amount when she arrives in Saudi Arabia. And, of course you are friends with the horse owner.

Izabella: How do you know all this?

Oleg: It's not us Izabella. Representatives from Prince Azid have found this out for us. It is there for you Izabella, that is all we say. *(expansive opening of arms, hands)*

Izabella: It is a very persuasive price. *Affirmation*

Yakov: We would not have approached you if it had not been so, Izabella. *Reference – looks toward Oleg, for affirmation.*

_____Curtain_____

Act Three: Scene One: Curtain open.

Persuasion's Price – double bedroom – Anton's

Carin enters with Vicky and case – Vicky leaves. Calls her boss. At Trellis and Vine Bedroom. Enters stage left.

Carin enters, on phone. Listens intently, for ten seconds.

Carin: Okay, Veronica, I've booked for the night. A single and double. *Pause.* We're to visit his mother tomorrow, before we go back, yep. *Pause. Alarm, in raised voice* - You what - Veronica? *Pause.* Yes. He's not gay, but I've a partner, thank you. *Longer pause.* The department may've sanctioned an advance in my relationship beyond that of PA – doesn't mean I have to does it? *Pause.*

I get it – I've to see it as career advancement, to share a bed with Anton Carter, but only because I'm scared of being alone in a pub's bedroom! *Pause.* Veronica, I'm in a position to monitor the activities of Taras Kedrov, fair enough. Sleeping with his son goes beyond that line of duty. *Pause.* I can assure you there's not going to be any intimacy. Why would any woman want to be seen as getting a promotion from - *hears Anton's approach?* Got to go. *Anton enters stage left.*

Anton: I take it this is my bedroom?

Carin: Unless, you prefer a single bedroom, that's all there is.

Anton: Okay, that's fine by me. Father and Izabella are back to Brodham. I've got to catch up on some paperwork, in the bar. You're welcome to join me or -

Carin: Or, I can sit on my own in a single bedroom and listen to the owls, which scare me.

Anton: No, I didn't mean it like that. I meant that I probably won't be good company. *Slight pause.* Do they. I mean, really scare you?

Carin: It might sound odd, but in a strange country pub - middle of nowhere. *Pause.* Anton, could I ask a favour?

Anton: Yes, if you want an early night, it's alright by me.

Carin: It's not that, but, Anton, now, you've a double bed. You understand I'm in a relationship. Um, you do understand. Would you mind if I asked to share your bed? I mean to share the bed for sleep – nothing more! Do really need a good night's sleep and those owls, they're scary, and they'll keep me awake.

Anton: But what if my snoring keeps you awake?

Carin: Take a chance on that. No, it means you'll have a PA, whose well rested, for tomorrow. No, it will mean, you'll have a PA, who's well rested, for tomorrow. Can I take that as a yes with conditions firmly in place?

Anton: But it just seems ridiculous to be scared of owls. If you want, yes. You've not answered me about whether you'll join me in the bar, though?

Carin: After I've unpacked. *Smiles at Anton.* I can take it – P Aing's, finished   for the day?

Anton: You can. *Smiles back.*

_____Curtain_____

Act Three: Scene Two: Scene Two:

– *Curtain opens on same, with bedside light on. Anton is in bed, asleep. Carin, enters in dressing gown. Only light, is a bedside table light next to where Anton sleeps. Carin goes over to Anton's side. Looks at him sleeping, smiles and switches light off. Returns to own side of bed, removes dressing gown, and places on hook on door. An owl is heard and she gets discretely into bed next to Anton. Turns away. They sleep. Curtain closes for a few seconds and opens again, to mark passage of time. Anton, already turned toward Carin places right arm around her and draws her close, while calling out -*

Anton: Petra, Petra, I love you.

Carin: *Removes arm. Sits up in bed* Anton, I'm not Petra! *Anton pulls back duvet. Carin's night dress is up above her waist. She pulls this down. She's wearing black knickers.*

Anton: I'm sorry – I don't know what happened. I mean….

Carin: Anton. It's a good thing I'm wearing M& S knickers. *Pause.* Petra, might be disappointed, not to be here.

Anton: Don't know what happened, Carin. Are you okay?

Carin: *Turns and smiles toward Anton.* Very much awake thanks to you. What time is it? *Draws knees up – tucks in nightdress demurely. Anton switches on bedside light and looks at watch on table.*

Anton: It's seven thirty.

Carin: Really? Is it that time? Better get back to my bedroom. I'm alright, Anton. *Smiles.* I mean it won't look good seen together like this. The owls have gone and …

Anton: Really sorry about that. Don't know what happened. I was dreaming.

Carin: Sorry, I' m not Petra. It's okay I've slept pretty well. Petra missed out it seems, though Anton. *Carin turns and smiles. Gets out of bed – allows view of legs for Anton and fetches dressing gown from door hook and puts on.*

Carin: I arranged an eight thirty call. It's probably best I'm in my own bed – don't you think? *And leaves stage left.*

───────────── Curtain ─────────────

Act Four:

At Heron Tower ("Pre" – curtain rise; narrator Jason Whatley nonchalantly walks on, stage right, with work bag. Centre stage stops. Puts, work bag, down on to stage floor; removes, furled Heron Tower banner. *Silver background with red "Heron Tower," logo.* Unfurls, above head "Heron Tower," banner for audience, to see. Re-furls and replaces in bag. Exits stage left

* music play prior to narrator entrance. Beethoven's Turkish March – Ruin of Athens Incidental Music, op.113- *

_____Curtain rise_____

Stage scene: Lounge / dining area in penthouse. Centre stage back wall a Venetian blind covered window. Carpeted front to window. Modern style wall prints, either side. Stage left – dining table - Jane Albright, at table head, with two civil servants. Stage right – larger, easy chair for Julian Reynolds; coffee table – between two easy chairs for Anton and Carin. Door entrances stage right and left.

Head of dining table, stage left, Jane Albright, seated and is seen gathering up papers; shutting down an iPad. On her left, two civil servants, who face, settee group of three, stage right, who are - Tom Draycot, Junior minister (light blue suit) in easy chair, rather than arm chair, angled toward audience, but back, to Jane. Anton and Carin, stage right of Tom. Chairs positioned around a coffee table. Tom, with opened lap top. Anton, seated faces both Tom and Jane. Carin with folders and iPhone in hand, left of Anton, to face audience, more directly.

Tom Draycot, is stood, as curtain rises, nods head, as if in agreement and chats to Jane, before being handed document by Jane. Phone, held, in left hand, he walks across – gives document to Anton; places phone on table and is speaking lines before sitting. Anton, opens, document briefly glances at, stapled document, and hands to Carin. Looks at her iPhone to check details.

Tom Draycot: Everything's in order. *Anton smiles.* We've, contractors, assigned with five participant councils, for our twinned car park programme. *(picks up phone)* - A good deal for our nation and your fund holders. *Looks at phone.* I've, to be back in the house by five. *second civil servant, away from Jane, closes folder, places it in bag on table.* We've a motion, to ban all city centre diesal vehicles. It won't go through this time - keeps the pot boiling, so to speak. Government's proposed plans of - forty per cent reduction in parking fees. That's for electric vehicles; a nudge in the right direction.

Anton: *Turns toward Carin.* Carin are we good to go?

Carin: It all matches up. *Tom stands up. They follow. Second civil servant, away from Jane, gets up; preparatory to accompany to leave with Tom Draycot.*

Tom: So good to meet with you and Carin. *Shakes both their hands. Second civil servant, walks across and shuts down lap top/ places in case and accompanies Tom, toward exit stage left. Anton and Carin follow – Jane Albright, cuts in, but before they reach table, with -*

Jane Albright: One moment Mr Carter. We would like you to remain a while longer. *Door stage right opens. Reynolds enters. Dark suited – upright military bearing. Smiles toward Jane Albright. Door remains open* It's been very nice meting you and Carin. This is Julian Reynolds from Intelligence, he requested to meet up, to discuss matters of security. *Reynolds: stands to one side, to allow, two dark suited body guards to enter (either, male or female), who move to stand each side of Venetian blind window, centre back stage wall.* Possible *additional role for Luke, with suit, from Act one.*

Jane Albright: You understand. Mr Carter, it will be a matter of national interest. *Jane Albright, and remaining civil servant, stand up.*

Anton: Really? I was given to understand our meeting was about my role in a government funded project. Nothing else.

Jane Albright: Yes, Mr Carter, but intelligence services are part of government, you understand. We'll leave you, in their capable hands. *Jane Albright and remaining civil servant stand up. Civil servant clears away table, whilst Jane, moves from table toward Anton and Carin. Civil servant, stands discreet distance behind her boss; and both are clear of table when three security department officials enter. Two men and smart suited young woman; * bag with VDU screen. The men sit at the table vacated by Jane and civil servant. Both with lap top bags. Casual, geek smart, not suited. Proceed to open bags and place lap tops on table. Third official, smart suited, skirted young woman, * who moves front of stage with VDU screen. Places, stage front. Walks back to move table forward, to support screen, and face, where Anton ad Reynolds are to sit.*

Carin: What's going on?

Reynolds: It's alright, my dear; but perhaps you'd like to wait in the next room. We need to talk with Mr Carter. *Julian Reynolds introduces himself to Anton, with outstretched hand. Anton does not respond to proffered hand. Julian withdraws hand – but not perturbed.*

Reynolds: Reynolds, Julian Reynolds, security services.

Anton: Carin can stay. *Jane Albright, walks toward Carin, briefly, takes arm, smiles, removes hand.*

Reynolds: We need to talk, in strictest confidence, you understand. Ministers and politicians come and go, it is true, but we remain to keep the ship on, course *(smiles) Carin looks to Anton for direction. Jane Albright holds out hand to direct away. Skirt suited civil servant joins other two on table – having set up the VDU screen. One shows her screen and converse about picture.*

Jane Albright: Come with me, Carin. A routine security matter, which needs to be resolved, that's all. We can visit the apartment rooms. It's, as they say - how the other half live.

Carin: I'm alright Anton. *Smiles and leaves with animated, Jane. Civil servant, following.*

Reynolds: We are, as Jane has mentioned, part of government, but we don't hog the limelight, you understand.

Reynolds, points to chairs and settee. Anton, seats himself. Keeps, two window detail, in view. Reynolds, opposite, with chair slightly angled toward audience.

Anton: What do you want and why do I warrant this reception? *Reynolds places phone on table.*

Reynolds: Good question and I can answer that, Anton. May, I call you, Anton.

Anton: Does it matter? No doubt you hold information, about me. Guess, you could address me by file reference number.

Reynolds: Anton, Anton, we need to work together, and with your father, in a mutually beneficial way, you must understand – for both your family, and government primary need. We're just workers in the field. No reason for us not to be on amicable terms, is there?

Anton: I'll leave my response on file, if you don't mind, Julian.

Reynolds – *gives a half – smile and raises his hand.* That's alright. *Expansively raises hand* - Alison, load the footage to view on main screen, will you? *Alison stands up.*

Alison: From the NEC do you mean, Julian?

Alison, walks across, with remote, and stands to left of Reynolds.

Reynolds: Yes, for starters. *Alison, makes selection on remote and points to screen. Anton looks toward VDU screen and contemplates. Feigns interest, with hand on chin. Removes after video starts.*

Anton: So? So, what! A video, of a stall at the NEC

Reynolds: Your father's.

Anton: Could be.

Reynolds: It is, I assure you. Let it run Alison. *They continue to view screen. Slight pause.*

Reynolds: *Raises hand to point toward screen.* That marine valve you see displayed, was intercepted at Southampton. A sizeable quantity of cocaine was seized by Customs. No doubt about its origin. *Points to screen.* You will know about this?

Anton: I know little about my father's business.

Reynolds: Cocaine contained within a valve, bound for China, via Saudi Arabia. And, what's more, traced further back. Marine valves first stored in barns at a farm, arrived from Holland. Engineered there, and we understand, were first loaded with cocaine. *Pauses.*

That valve, we are certain came from your father's stall. Opened by Customs, on our instructions, with container investigation at Southampton docks. Containers bound for Saudi Arabia and China. We can trace back to *(points toward screen)* even to the farm where it was stored.

Alison: It's called Linton Farm, Julian.

Reynolds: Thanks for that, Alison. Yes, Linton Farm and our understanding is that your father leased three barns, on the farm. *(Pause -raised hand, slow wave to right – to accentuate knowledge)*

Anton, you see, we know, who you are. *pause* British interests stretch worldwide, of course. China, Saudi Arabia, you won't be surprised to know, are very much on our radar. *Pause.* We've no evidence of your father selling cocaine in the UK. He would be wise not to.

Serendipitously, for your sakes, authority's been allowed for cocaine consignments, to slip, into a demanding China market. To counter cyber - attack into Britain's intellectual property, an ever present - threat. This action in concurrence with security policy: cocaine – with certain chemical drug supply export, is not presently disapproved of, you understand. That's to main land China. Ready supply for a market where, cocaine addiction has its uses.

Happenstance, is that Anton, your father's trucks, carry more legitimate goods than illegal. State interest, requires, an off - grid transport system, for overseas commitments, and, luckily for your father, his transport logistics, conveniently meet that requirement.

Anton: my father would have had no choice, at trade fairs, when approached by the might of China. You must see that.

Reynolds: That – that, Anton, is open to conjecture. We can, arrive at an understanding. You, meet up with your father?

Anton: Occasionally.

Reynolds: need to prioritize, that. Explain our chat; that business continuation, of any kind, depends on cooperation. Government, has present need, to dispatch anonymously, overseas. And, as explained, your father's storage facility, at Linton Farm, coupled with transport hubs overseas, meet with requirement. *Picks up smart phone.*

Anton: You want me to explain, and get agreement? *Reynolds taps phone to bring up phone number.*

Reynolds: Yes, yes, that's exactly it. Persuade him to accept - if he wants to continue doing anything meaningful businesswise - right Anton? Here's a secure number you can find me at, Anton Carter or do you prefer Kedrov – hum? *Takes from top pocket of suit jacket, a sticky note pad, pen. Hand's pen and notepad to Anton.* Write this down will you, please Anton– *Anton places pad on coffee table*

Reynolds: *satisfied smile on face – reads out from phone.* Two, two, seven, seven, six, zero, six, nine. You, Mr Carter, I believe will be able to commit this to memory. It's not a difficult selection.

Anton: Right. *Anton having written down numbers silently reads them out*

Reynolds: When you feel confident – tear it up. *Anton holds the note up before tearing it into four pieces.*

_____Curtain fall_____

Interval

Fifteen-minute interval.

Before curtain open and whilst audience are nearly settled:

Narrator, Jason Whatley: enters stage right with bicycle – Jason, attired in cycle gear/crash hat. Between cycle frame is a board sign – luminescent orange wording, on black background – "Izabella's Office," **for both sides of board.** Jason, on entry, stage left – wipes forehead – takes out mobile phone from breast pocket. Engrossed in phone, whilst pushing bike across stage.

Before he reaches stage left, stops and places phone back in breast pocket; turns cycle around, to scoot leisurely back the way came and stops before stage right. Wipes, forehead and mounts cycle, prior to exit stage right.

Act Five:

Izabella's office: Izabella is sat at desk - Taras – on phone centre stage.

Izabella: You must do something Taras. My business is interfered with.

Taras: Yes, yes Izabella, *looks away from phone.* I know, okay, they've held your crates for two weeks. Police forensics needed to look at them, but afterwards, they said, we can have them back. It will be soon. There's nothing more I can do cherie. *Sits down in chair, with small table, stage right, of desk. Places phone on table.*

Izabella: It's because, Taras, you're Russian. Discrimination, because of a perfume bottle and Novichok. You do see that don't you?

Taras: Vivid imagination, cherie. Maybe, maybe not. It is complicated, anyhow. *Expansive gesture with hands.* Gypsies in the lane were found to have handled crates and market traders they were suspicious - where are cosmetics from? I know no more, cherie – I would tell you, if I did.

Izabella: Five Taras, - five of my crates were taken from the warehouse. Why didn't Mr Leadley report this to the police?

Taras: They sawed through the padlock, and replaced it to make it look okay.

Izabella: And the door wasn't locked?

Taras: Perhaps the door was left open, cherie. It might've been worse. *Eva knocks on door, stage left.*

Taras: Yes! Eva enters. *A young woman, enters stage left. Jeans, smock top, tied back hair. Approaches desk.*

Eva: Izabella, what shall I do with the listings for the products, that are with the police? Listing numbers are low.

Izabella: *(picks up inventory from desk)* These are the ones affected. You will need, Eva, to put all these to unavailable. *Hands list to Eva, who takes it. Izabella then – dismissively.*

Izabella: *dismissively.* I may not list them again, anyway. *Eva, looks toward Taras*

Taras: Eva, do as Izabella, says. It's not for me to interfere.

Eva: Yes, Mr Kedrov. Is that all?

Izabella: For now - and, Eva -

Eva: Yes, Izabella?

Izabella: We need to speak about a matter, later. You know what I mean?

Eva: Yes, Izabella.

Izabella: I will call you.

Leaves with inventory. Greensleeves music ring tone on Taras's mobile, starts.

Taras: Ah, I so love this old English song. *(picks up mobile)* – "yes," *Pause.* Taras Kedrov speaking – *pause* – no, no sergeant it is no bother. Not at all inconvenient, and the crates? have been looked at. *Pause.* Yes, I can send a van to collect them. That's so helpful. Thank you for calling – *pause* – yes, I understand it was procedure, yes, yes, quite alright – goodbye. The gods have been favourable to me *(aside to audience)*

Taras: The police have released your cosmetics, Izabella.

Izabella: And, I should think so, they'd no business to hold them. It's good, I will be able to contact Annetta. I promised to let her see samples. *(Izabella, leans forward and raises herself from the* chair) *Taras's smile activated by view of shapely thighs – revealed when she kneels, to pick up a handbag – also in relief at return of cosmetics.*

Izabella: I need the office for a while.

Taras: Of course, cherie. I will let you know the moment that we have your cosmetics back in store. *Walks to stage right exit. Izabella picks up phone. Presses button. Pauses for response.*

Izabella: I would like to see you now. *Pause.* Yes, now. You can put that work on hold. *Shortly afterwards door opens, stage left; Izabella, is sat at desk, looking through a catalogue, which she puts down and picks up smart phone/iPad.*

Eva: You want to see me, Izabella?

Izabella: Yes, and you know why. You are late for a second time. Twenty pounds will be taken from your salary - this week. *Eva, walks across to front of desk.*

Izabella: Sit down. *Before sitting down Eva, starts talking.*

Eva: ---- *(exclamatory)* But Izabella, it's my turn to pay the rent - that will be hard! *Eva, sits in chair front of desk.*

Izabella: *(Looks up from phone/ iPad)* Then, you should have thought about consequence, for being late, then? *Izabella, accesses long ruler from behind desk; places on front before getting up, to walk out.*

Izabella: Stand up, please. There is a solution. *(Eva, stands)*

Eva: And I will not have to lose twenty pounds, from my wage?

Izabella. That's right. *Izabella, reaches out to touch Eva's right buttock.* Three. Just three on here. and you can keep the twenty pounds. Alright?

Eva: And no wage deduction?

Izabella: Turn around. *(Eva turns to face desk. Izabella picks up ruler)*

Lean over the desk for me. **(curtain begins to fall** – *Izabella, is seen to raise arm, whilst holding long ruler)* Immediately, **curtain fall** *covers table height three spaced yelps are heard coming from Eva.*

Five second break, before initial slow speed, paced and then more rapid **curtain rise/open.**

Izabella is stood back with long ruler held in right hand. Held at top with left hand. She strokes the ruler where it has met Eva's bottom and then reaches out to pass an opened tissue box from desk. Eva holds her bottom, with right hand – Eva, wipes away tears. Plucks three tissues from box.

Izabella: It was not so bad. I have some cream from a new collection. You can be a first customer to try it, and write a good review.

Izabella: Do not be late again. I cannot promise a simple punishment like this again.

Eva: No wage deduction.

Izabella: No wage deduction. You are good girl. Now you can pay the rent, yes. Don't say to anyone, about this. You will want to be a model for our new winter range?

Eva: Yes, yes, of course Izabella.

Izabella: There'll be no opportunities to model clothes, if you tell anyone. I wouldn't like to lose you, Eva, okay?

Eva: Yes, Izabella. Thank you.

Izabella walks across to unlock the office door, whilst Eva reties belt around her jeans. A smile of satisfaction remains on Izabella's face as Eva returns to the main office.

Shortly afterwards there's a call on Izabella's mobile.

Izabella: Hello. *Pause.* Yes, he is expected. Send him in. - *door opens shortly afterwards an*d *Oleg enters. Stage left.*

Oleg: Good afternoon Izabella. It is…

Izabella: Cut the small talk, Oleg. What progress has been made

Oleg: Progress is good, Izabella. May I sit down first? *Izabella points toward a chair.*

Izabella: And what progress, is that?

Oleg: For making available, where the girl exercises the horse, a first instalment is to be made of a hundred and fifty thousand pounds. You need, Izabella, to find out exact days and times that she visits, and where the postmistress stables this horse, called Cleopatra. Prince Azid, though has decided not to buy the horse.

Izabella: But?

Oleg: No, Izabella, it's okay! Arrangements, are still for visitors to stay, near to the post office.

Izabella: And how Oleg, how does that come about?

Oleg: It is straightforward, don't worry; postmistress, Annetta Hastings has stable yard space, for motor home visitors. Our special visitors stay there, in their Motor Home, and they snatch the girl, when visiting the horse. For second instalment, as I've said, you need, Izabella, to have information about when the girl is there.

Izabella: It's that simple?

Oleg: You maybe, can show understanding to Miss Hastings, if she speaks about the sale falling through. How the hire out of space for Motor Homes must be helpful for the running of the shop

Izabella: I could be interested in buying the horse myself.

Oleg: That's such a good idea, Izabella. We knew that you could build a good relationship with this woman.

Izabella: And for the third instalment?

Oleg: When the girl is taken in the Motor Home to board a private jet. The final one, when she arrives at the prince's palace.

Izabella: It is persuasive, so far. And if she doesn't get there?

Oleg: Each step will have been accredited. You cannot be expected to do more, than that and Izabella, you have contacts in high places, which will see that you are protected.

Izabella: You talk about my friendship with the President – Oleg, Taras is not to know.

Oleg: No intention of telling Taras, anything. It's good for everyone, Izabella, you share a special friendship with the president and he is friends also with Prince Azid. We have a very good contract set up; do you not think Izabella?

Izabella: Payment is from a legitimate bank?

Oleg: Middle Eastern oil, speaks, a special language to banks. Have no worries, Izabella, it will be a British bank. Invoices, will be prepared, for payment of high value gems - sent to the Prince's office. A quarter of a million pounds is not such a large sum. It will be seen as, every day for an oil rich, middle eastern prince, do you not think? It is not business; a bank will easily turn away from.

_____Curtain_____

Act Six: Trellis and Vine

Carin's informed about Motor Home. Boxed Reception desk adjoins bar. Immediate to stage right entrance. Trellis fence on back wall, with grape vine near; entrance stage right. Carol, is behind bar. Floor plan. Three bar stools. Stage floor, front of bar; five card table sized tables. Three, stage right, with three/four chairs. Covered in white table cloths. Two tables and chairs stage left, with two chairs facing, one another. Veronica Gates. Carin's secret service boss sat at table, nearest to bar.

Show ground photos, staggered, on stage back wall, each side of bar – which is off set centre, toward stage left.

Leather strapped, hanging wall brasses – frame bar, on either side. Copper warming pan, stage left – back wall. Behind bar, Three, miniature bulls/sheep with rosettes on wall plinths, intermingled with bar wall bottles, which is glass backed. Empty beer mugs, trays of glasses – wine/empty squash glasses/straws are spaced around the bar, on trays. Tankards hang from bar overhang. After Carin's entrance, Carol's occupied with glass collection from bar top.

Veronica Gates, Carin's secret service boss, is sat at one of two chaired tables, stage left – with half full glass, of white wine. Opposite, near full, white wine glass. On phone, which she places on table with Carin's arrival. Nearest table has a wine glass/ Guinness tumbler plus two sandwich plates, with small knives/ scrunched paper napkins.

Narrator, is sat at bar - downs half pint, looks at watch, before getting up from stool. Walks to dart board – back wall stage left – pulls out three darts steps back and throws them at board, then walks to exit stage right – not, before standing back to allow Carin to enter stage right. George, is in reception desk area and calls out. Carol is in bar area, drying, polishing glasses from bowl of soapy water – not visible to audience.

George: Oh, Miss Hanson. *Carin stops.*

Carol: A Miss Gates is here to see you.

Carin: Really.

George: She's, Just over there. *Motions with hand to where Veronica's sat.*

Carin: Thanks. *Walks across to table.*

Carin: What if Anton sees us?

Veronica: *Inspecting menu. Turns to look at Carin, but does not get up. Plonk's menu down.*

Veronica: I've taken the liberty to order you a drink, Carin. Two women are free to talk in a bar – are they not? We've urgent information, and a proposition to make, which - is best discussed, person to person. Sit down Carin. *Carin sits across from Veronica, who is stage left to Carin. Carin's chair angled more to front stage and audience.*

Carin: A proposition to do what? *Carol, at this point, leaves bar to clear glasses/plates/knives and napkins from adjoining table to that of Veronica and Carin.*

Suzi: *– Asian accented voice from back stage -kitchen area'*

    George, George You're needed here - now!

George: Right with you Suz. *Closes, red leather type hard back guest book. Reaches out and returns to plinth – front of reception area. Smiles for benefit of Carin and Veronica.* On my way.

Exits, backstage from bar area.

Veronica: An opportunity for career advancement, Carin. We know you're doing vital work in the field monitoring, Anton and Taras Kedrov, but something has happened, which upsets the department's interface of services we need from the Kedrovs'

Carin: And what is that Veronica?

Veronica: One moment – *waits for Carol to return to bar area. Carol places tray on bar. Returns to bar and adds glasses to tray before exit through back stage with tray of glasses knives and plates to kitchen.*

Veronica: Carin, there's another young woman, who works at the Trellis and Vine.

Carin: Vicky?

Veronica: You know her?

Carin: Vicky's, daughter of the farmer that leases barns to the Kedrov's

Veronica: Yes, well, recent phone monitoring, between Taras Kedrov's associates, has shown that they're implicated in a plan to capture her.

Carin: What? That can't be true?

Veronica: Izabella has accepted a role, of intermediary to assist in the kidnap. Payment, made to her Hong Kong account.

Carin: Whose, behind it?

Veronica: A prince Azid, who attended the same university. A motor home's, in the area, tasked with a plan to kidnap Vicky; drive her to Bristol airport, and fly the girl, by private jet, to the Middle East.

Carin: Taras Kedrov - Anton and Izabella! They're all involved in this?

Veronica: No, no only the woman. But it interferes with future arrangements. Carin, it's a side issue that needs dealing with.

Carin: That's ghastly. I mean, a discovery that's only been made by accident, really.

Veronica: Yes, that's as maybe; *shrugs.* But it can be sorted. A more pressing matter, is your relationship, with Anton.

Carin: What do you mean – my relationship, with Anton. I'm his Personal Assistant.

No more!

Veronica: I've some, what maybe disappointing news, Carin. Simon, has been moonlighting, whilst you've been away.

Carin: had suspicions…

Veronica: That's good Carin. We need to know about these things. That, you're not disturbed by domestic affairs, whilst in the field. It's short notice, but there's promotion opportunity, if you can step away from that relationship.

Carin: To do what?

Veronica: Marry Anton.

Carin: What Veronica! That's crazy. I mean, I'm seen as his employee, and I might not be his type.

Veronica: But in an ideal role, as PA, do you not think? With a move to a yet more secure and influential level. Temporarily, yes but to gain their trust *(dismissive)* don't worry, Carin, we'll set up grounds for divorce, after say a year.

Carin: A temporary role?

Veronica: Yes, but immediately after marriage you'd step up a pay grade. *Pause.*

Need, an answer Carin. Simon has strayed from the porch, so to speak. You told me, earlier that you had your suspicions. We need, an answer? *Carin looks away – weighing up situation – makes decision.*

Carin: Okay, but it takes two to tango. I can't just pop the question. Might lose my job and all progress that's been made. You do see that?

Veronica: Yep, obviously, a suitable moment, needs to be picked. A degree of subtlety, which we know you're capable of, is needed Carin and that is one reason, you were chosen to infiltrate. There's much for Anton Carter, or Kedrov to lose, in our bringing his father to justice, but there are issues.

Carin: What issues? Are you saying Veronica, that Taras Kedrov is beyond the law?

Veronica: British law will pursue British citizens, who transgress. With matters of international diplomacy, other rules can be instigated. None of this Carin, will ever be allowed near the media. There's no worry on that score.

Carin: I should think not.

Veronica: You enjoy benefit from a higher grade if, you're prepared to go forward, with marriage to Anton, and - in no longer than a year - we'll find reasons for divorce.

Carin: Alright, Veronica, if needs must. *Veronica, picks up phone – on table and gets up.*

Veronica: It's probably better that I'm not seen with you, Carin. *Moves away. Anton appears in doorway to bar, stage right – audience can see that his right coat shoulder is bloodied*

Anton: Carin, *he calls across, on spotting her at the table* "Carin, need you now!" *– calls out.*

Veronica: You'd better see what he wants, Carin?

Audience only, see Anton grasp his right shoulder – is holding green St John's type First aid box, in right hand.

__________

Act Seven:

Scene – (props required – two light weight bedroom chairs – on curtain rise) Same double bedroom as in Act Two: Scene Three.

Scene: Carin and Anton enter. Stage right. Carin now carries first aid box.

Carin: Who did this to you? Whatever happened., Anton, you'll need to take your coat off, if I'm to wrap a dressing around it. *Carin places first aid box on floor. Helps Anton remove blazer. Sits Anton on chair. Out of sight of Anton, places jacket lovingly on bed before fetching second chair, to position same side as Anton's shoulder wound. Retrieves first aid box from floor.*

Anton: Never heard a shot. Just parked up, in the supermarket car park and the window just opened, on its own accord. Must have accessed the cars system. Leant forward and felt, a searing pain. Luckily, the bullet scraped my shoulder and went into the seat. Wouldn't've managed the drive here, otherwise.

Carin: But who would do this to you? *Carin opens first aid box*

Anton: Father has enemies. *Carin has opened First aid box and prepares to wrap bandage around wound.*

Carin: You need to go to A&E. A medical professional, needs to look at it, to prevent infection. And Anton, I've something to tell you. I work for the security services.

Anton: What security services? What do you mean? – 'You're a spy!'

Carin: Not quite that straightforward. But there's inter – state action and I was placed…'

Anton: Like a sleeper?'

Carin: No, not, in a destructive way. But yes, like a sleeper, but I'm awakened, now. Look - Anton, I need to take you to A &E for proper medical attention.

Anton: how do I explain the injury? Won't the police get involved? And why are you telling me this?

Carin: The police kind of know already. *Carin smiles.* And … I more than just care for you. Look. I'll alert the hospital authority. Questions, about the wound won't be asked. I'm on your side Anton. You want to extricate your father from his mafia life – style?'

Anton: You know everything then? *Anton winces with pain from arm.*

Carin: Oh. Anton. *Carin, momentarily breaks away from her executive demeanour – reaches across, to touch Anton's arm*

'You're a good person to work for. It's terrible. I want to stay in this role, if you can accept my appointment was to ensure the Department of Transport was not at risk from exposure.

Anton: Exposure to the risk of having signed a contract with the son of a known gangster?

Carin: I can assist with the protection of legitimate businesses. And you are valuable, to the department. You've business and negotiating skills, that your father lacks.

Anton: What happens, when father's, told who you really are – or represent?

Carin: I've a proposition, which I'm happy with, if you are, which gets round this. Your father mightn't be happy – but then perhaps, he might?

Anton: And what's that?

Carin: That we marry Anton. It happens all the time, doesn't It? Boss marries secretary, situation. From your father's and Izabella's point of view, it would bring confidence to the situation. We'd sign, in the registry – like, "friends forever," rather than go serious.

Anton: You're acting under orders, then? I've news for you, Carin, Izabella plans to return to Vladivostok. *Carin's words do not really resonate, immediately.* "Marry?" You'd be happy to be married to the son of a gangster.

Carin: Very happy for us to be married.

Anton: I've my own confession to make.

Carin: What's that? – you're already married?

Anton: No. Nothing like that. Remember, Carin, that call of "Petra," in my sleep.

Carin: Do I? Do I? Do I remember that? Not something a woman's likely to forget, Anton. Well, what about Petra?

Anton: It wasn't Petra, it was you; I mean, I mean, I was dreaming about you, Carin. Then, *pause,* when I woke, I called, "Petra," to make it seem that I was dreaming about someone else.

Carin: Oh! They want it to be a marriage of convenience.

Anton: They, being your superiors?

Carin: It was, suggested, I should sleep in your bed.

Anton: In the line of duty, that is?

Carin: But it wasn't like that for me, Anton.

Anton: They believed, and still believe - you're acting out a professional role?

Carin: Yes, but I decided quite early, once I knew the risks, you were taking that –

Anton: Come here. *Carin gets out of chair – Anton, also*

Carin: I've got to get you to hospital. *They kiss –*

Anton: You will marry me then – I'm the one that's supposed to ask!

Carin: Of course, Anton. *Kissing progresses, before Carin breaks away.*

Carin: There's something else, Anton.

Anton: To do with father?

Carin: No, it's Izabella. You should know. *Sits back down* It's about Vicky, the Leadley's daughter.

Anton: Yes. What about Vicky? Vicky from Linton farm. What about her?

Carin: Izabella's set herself up as an intermediary, for a kidnap attempt.

Anton: What! by whom?

Carin: Vicky's a target for a certain Prince Azid. Apparently, they went to the same university and Izabella has a background of slave trafficking. She was approached by Oleg and Yakov, who'd found a site on the dark web, which advertises capture payment, for people snatchers. They recognized Vicky, was out there. Money's already been transferred to Izabella's Hong Kong bank account.

Anton: That means Izabella will be arrested for her part in this?

Carin: Not exactly. It's just not, in the department's interest, for this to enter the public domain. It could snarl up arrangements planned between state and your father, over assisted trade routes, useful for overseas transport. Yes, the kidnap must be stopped, but beyond that… look I need to get you to hospital. *Phone rings. Carin takes it from suit pocket, sounds three times. Looks at it. Turns to Anton.*

Carin: It's from the department. *Pause*

Anton: Are you going to answer? *Carin, nods head slowly, and answers.*

Carin: Hi. *Pause.*

Carin: Now - you mean it's in progress, as we speak. *Pause.*

Carin: Right. Is there uniform presence? *Pause.* but there's been no intervention, are you sure?

Carin: Right, I'll get right down there. Oh, the answers yes. *Pause.* Yes, to that. *Pause.* That's *right. Looks, smilingly toward Anton, Pause.*

Carin: Talk later.

Carin: Kidnap's about to take place. Apparently, a trace put on a camper van, matched payment back to the prince. It's at West Frampton Post Office.

Anton: Really?

Carin: I can chauffeur you to the hospital it's on the way. Can you walk alright, Anton?

Anton: It's my shoulder – not my legs.

Curtain

Narrator walks across stage left to right front of closed curtain, carrying sign on pole. Turned away from audience. Stops mid stage. Realizes sign is turned wrong way and reverses it. Sign – reads – **West Frampton Post office.** Continues walking off stage – stage left

Act Eight:

Curtain rises on shop area of Frampton Post office. Danny and Annetta Hastings. Annetta, hands packets over counter, to Danny, who places them in postal bag. Annetta, then fills in with ballpoint, paper to hand to Danny.

(Design feature - ease of adaptation, from bar, at Trellis and Vine, to postal counter front – upstage.

Post office entrance is at stage left.

Danny is stood in front of post office counter with Annetta Hastings behind. Danny is taking packets to place in postal bag.

Danny: You're not selling Cleopatra then Miss Hastings?

Annetta: No. the sale's fallen through, Danny. You're not interested, are you?

Danny: You're joking. Bet Vicky would like to own Cleopatra. Don't suppose that she'll mind - sales fallen through. She'll get to ride more… *doorbell rings, stage left. Carin enters. Annetta stops writing. Calls across*

Annetta: If you've a letter to post, you'd better be quick.

Carin: No, I'm here to see Vicky.

Annetta: She's out on my horse by now, I expect. *Carin walks to stage right – removes Police Inspector ID card from inside jacket suit pocket. Danny moves to stage right away from counter position.*

Carin: Inspector Hampton. *Holds opened ID card wallet up to glass. Annetta looks at opened wallet card.*

Annetta: She's not in trouble, Inspector, is she? *Danny's keen to leave.*

Danny: Best be on my way then.

Carin: One moment. I noticed, that the Motor Home's no longer here.

Annetta: Possibly, I mean they're due to leave. *Goes to window at back of office. Returns,*

Annetta: No, you're right, they've left. Vicky will be out with Cleopatra. You'll most likely have to wait, if you want to talk with her. *Carin turns to Danny.*

Carin: I'd like you to check for me, whether the horse is still stabled. Can you do that?

Annetta: That's unlikely. She'll be away by now.

Danny: You want me to drive down to the stables?

Carin: Yes. Let us know, as soon as you get there.

Danny: Like, how. *Carin, turns to Annetta*

Carin: Can you see the stables from your back window?

Annetta: usually watch out for Vicky's return. *Carin turning to Danny.*

Carin: When you get there, wave if the horse's stabled and there's no Vicky, I need to know? And will need your further assistance.

Danny: Sure, can do. *Hands postal bag back through to Annetta.* Okay, if that's what you want. *Danny exits stage left — removes keys from shorts, on walk to exit.*

Annetta: It's unlikely, that she's still there. Be cantering across those fields. Like, wish I could. *(doorbell rings. Alan Whatley, enters with parcel to post)*

Annetta: You're in luck, Danny's still here. *(narrator walks across and places parcel on scales. Sound of postal van starting*

63

Narrator: Thought I'd missed him. He's driving off, isn't he?

Annetta: No, he'll be back. What's inside?

Alan: Just books.

Annetta: Right. That'll be three thirty – second class or –

Alan: Second class will be fine. *Hands over five - pound note. Annetta sticks label on and gives change.*

Alan: Thanks. *Alan Whatley, leaves.*

Carin: Is the postman there yet? Annetta goes to window.

Annetta: Yes, Danny's just opened the gate and's walking to the stable. *Pause.* He's waving. That's most unusual, Vicky's usually away by now. *Carin's on phone. Has moved more to stage front.*

Carin: Sergeant. *Pause.* Right: That Motor Home. *Pause.* Yes, with the trace. Get traffic to halt, it before the M4, will you? I'll follow up. Make sure the occupants only believe it to be a safety check when stopped. *Pause.* Yes, delay, entry, beyond exterior tyre checks, until I get there, understood. *Pause.* Keep me up to date with sat nav direction, once vehicle is halted

Annetta: What's this all about? You don't think she's in the Motor Home

Carin: We've reason to believe so. Perhaps there's a perfectly innocent explanation

Annetta: I hope so

Carin: I'll need Danny to go with me.

Annetta: How do you mean? He's here to take the post. He's at work. He's at work!

Carin: Alternative arrangements can be made. Contact your collection supervisor for alternative arrangements. If, as we suspect, Vicky is in the Motor Home, then she will have reassurance with Danny with us to identify her.

Annetta: But you are delaying the Queen's Mail!

Carin: I'm sure the Queen will, be understanding about the situation.

Danny enters breathlessly.

Danny: Vicky's nowhere to be seen.

Carin: I want you to come with me. We've reason to believe, that she's in the Motor Home.

Danny: Why? How?

Carin: I'll explain. We need to leave now There's a trace on the Motor Home.

Danny: The Post?

Carin: Leave the van keys with Miss Hastings. She'll message for a replacement driver.

Miss Hastings, you have signed the official secrets act, haven't you?

Annetta: Yes.

Carin: Then this visit by me is to be considered, as such – secret - likewise, Danny. All that occurs today, is just between the three of us. Understood?

Danny: Right, I get you, about that, but not much else.

Annetta: If you say so Inspector, of course.

Curtain

Scene change music: Prokofiev Symphony No 1, Op.24 "Classical" 2nd Movement Larghetto (4.02)

Pre – curtain time, back stage, expands with Narrator's performance

Act Nine:

Narrator: Dressed in track suit – Jogs, on spot stage left, holding furled, two stick banners, under arm. Then to centre stage. Stops and takes banner from under arm – unfurls – message for audience - Lay by – near M4." Held, across chest, like exercise band.

Curtain rise

Scene – Front Motor home cab profile stage right – dotted lines denote layby –over – filled black litter bin – gold "Litter, lettered back stage right. Empty cans shimmer in hedge caught by spots. Tree/shrub back drop – three bar wooden rail, surround with one broken top rail stage left and one mid rail snapped away mid – stage. Two police, one centre stage with Vicky and one Motor Home occupant.

Vicky: Why've we been stopped?

First Police (M): It's routine, madam. *Police 2 – seen to kneel and check front tyre.*

Woman Motor Home Occupant: Our vehicle is legal. What is all this about? *Danny, enters stage left, followed by Carin. Vicky turns toward them.*

Vicky: What are you doing here?

Danny: Are you okay? *Appearance of Carin.*

Police 1: *Salutes.* Marm. Vehicle seems to be in order. – *Carin, acknowledges Police 1's salute.*

Vicky: Can't I go for a ride in a Motor Home? And you're Anton's…

Carin: Yes, but I also hold a special inspector position.

Danny: That's right Vicky, she came looking for you at Annetta's.

Motor Home 1: Vicky was enjoying a ride. We are testing our Motor Home, before we leave and invited Vicky for a ride. We were about to stop here to have tea and were forced into the layby. It is, as you English say, motoring pleasure.

Carin: That's, as maybe. We understand, that you had paid up, and left the site at West Frampton. *Driver of vehicle steps out of vehicle.*

Motor Home Occupant 1: Yes, but Vicky was enjoying a ride and we are about to return. (smiles) at Vicky.

Motor Home Driver 2: This is harassment. We have diplomatic immunity. This is bad for our country's relationship. We're holidaying, sightseeing village churches.

Carin: That's as maybe. *Turns to Vicky.* You're alright to come with us?

Vicky: Yes, but what's all the fuss?

Carin: I'll explain, in the car on the way to the farm. Your safety is our priority. And I'd appreciate not telling anyone about my true status.

Vicky: The farm? I've to exercise Cleopatra first!

Danny: - How am I, to get home? That was my last call before going back to the office?

Vicky: That's not a problem Danny, father's picking me up - just messaged him. He'll drop you off, no worries.

Carin: That's sorted then.

Curtain

Act Ten:

A day later.

Bar of Trellis and Vine. Carin with George at bar, polishing glasses on to a tray. Turns to Carin, who is sat stage right of George, on bar stool.

George: Mr Carter has his arm in a sling I noticed.

Carin: Yes. *iPhone rings*

Carin: you must excuse me, George.

Call from behind bar – kitchen area - GEORGE!

George: And me - it seems. *Carin gets up and walks to front of stage with phone.*

Carin, answers, phone.

Carin: Hi. *Pause.* Yes Veronica, *(nods head in affirmation)* the girl knows nothing about the kidnap. Apparently. asked about whether she liked to travel, but got no further. *Pause* Yep, Traffic stopped them at that point.

Danny enters stage right. Places parcel on bar. Spots Carin,

Carin: they have diplomatic immunity Veronica, and that's sufficient to get them off the hook? Really? *Carin realizing Danny has entered. turns toward him.*

Carin: Catch up with you. *Pause.* Bye. *Danny explodes with,*

Danny: Is that right, Inspector? They've got away with what they did?

Carin: Shh. Danny, I was a police inspector, just for that day. Official secrets Act.

Danny: That's criminal though - taking Vicky was a criminal offence, wasn't it?

Carin: Vicky's unaware that she's been targeted and was about to kidnapped, Danny?

Danny: No, I've not mentioned that, as you said.

Carin: Good. Then that's as far as it needs to go. *George returns.*

George: Just in time, Postman Danny – I have these to go. *Reaches under bar and produces parcels – with receipt to sign? Anton enters, with arm in sling, stage left.*

George: What has happened "**to**" you? *Addresses Anton - Carin intervenes on* "to."

Carin: It was a sporting accident.

George: What sport is that?

Carin: Polo

Anton: Just a clip of the shoulder, with a mallet? Never noticed really until after we'd finished. Slight splinter, that's all.

George: Sport of Kings. There you are – hands sheet/book to Danny, who leaves. *Another call of*– George –

George: *head turn in direction of call raised voice* - A minute, a minute! You'd like a drink, before I return to the kitchen.

Anton. What would you like? Turns to Carin.

Carin: Gin and tonic?

Anton: Yes, make that two gin and tonics.

George: Please sit down – I'll bring them over. You need to rest that arm.

Carin and Anton go to a table – front of stage – George dispenses two gins and cuts lemon. Place's gin and tonics on tray with half bottle of tonic.

Carin: I've so missed you, Anton. I've an appointment for you tomorrow. Vicky's safe you'll be glad to know. That plan to smuggle her away, in a Motor Home was foiled.

Anton: Perpetrators - now in uniformed police custody, then?

Carin: Not exactly. It's unlikely to lead to prosecution. Traffic stopped the vehicle, only shortly after they'd driven away with Vicky in the back. She was invited to see inside, drove off while they road tested the vehicle, supposedly, Luckily, she didn't realize she'd been kidnapped; although shown photos of Prince Azid's palace.

Anton: A middle eastern prince's palace? They'd have been stopped at customs – wouldn't they?

Vicky: They'd have hidden her away and managed coverage to access the airfield, before smuggling her aboard. No, it's complicated, but the main priority was achieved – to release her. how's that shoulder?' George arrives with tray of drinks.

Anton: too painful to sleep on that side, if that's what you mean.

George: There, (*beaming smile*) you two could be a honeymoon couple sat there. *Places tray, on table and passes drink first to Carin and then Anton.*

Anton: Just a business meeting George. Need to unwind. *George returns to bar greeted by another call from kitchen area –* 'George. I am not your cook this evening. It is my evening for dance class with Izabella and Annetta.

George: On my way, my love?

Anton: *Clutches arm.* It throbs with pain. *But does not get immediate sympathy from Carin.*

Anton: *makes to wince.* Painkillers numb it a bit. *Carin reaches out this time with sympathetic hand across table.*

Anton: No, it's not too bad. *Anton, now toughing it out.*

Carin: I feel bad about leaving you.

Anton: *smiles* Good. I wouldn't have it otherwise. *Anton's hand from good arm, reaches across. Carin, this time takes hold of it and cups it between both hands, momentarily.*

Anton: And Carin Hanson, shortly to be Mrs Carter, we hope. What is the appointment that you've arranged for me tomorrow?

Carin: I've arranged to visit father.

Anton: Does he know? That…?

Carin: Sort of *pause – head adjustment, for direct to eye contact -eyebrows raised, lowered to - break - to intent smile, for Anton.* Think he could. He brought me up, after mother died.

Anton: And what do you mean by that, exactly, Miss Hanson? *(adopts boss talk to Personal Assistant.)*

Carin: When, he knew that you'd lent me the use of a Range Rover, he said – "no man lends his car, to just any woman." I remember him smiling, quietly to himself, but thought nothing of it

Anton: You're not just any woman.

Carin: I might have been. One, in a stream of Personal Assistants to Anton Carter. Quite like the name Kedrov, by the way.

Anton: You never were and certainly aren't now. Here's to my appointment with Jerry. *Raises glass – takes sip.* We've met, at that office farewell party to chauffeur Henry. He arrived with your then boyfriend, Simon – and yes Simon! How's he going to take it?

Carin: He's not in my life now, Anton. He kind of hasn't been, for some time. You're not worried about Simon?'

Anton: Only, if you are, my love.

Carin: Well, I'm not. Hey, did you see the moon tilted on its back, when you arrived outside. That means we can relax, as well.

Anton: You're not superstitious, are you?

Carin: I believe, phases of the moon can affect us. It certainly can affect a woman's cycle and that's not forgetting the rise and fall of tides.

Anton: So, I've an appointment with your father, tomorrow. He knows about it?

Carin: Not completely. But it concerns you and me.

Anton: Of course. Now you've frightened me. He could say no. He might not want his beautiful daughter marrying into a family, like mine. *They kiss.*

Curtain

The End

Setting: Time and location.

Set in summer of 2019: Pre - curtain rise: A narrator enters and talks to audience.

Act 1: Scenes 2 to 3: A farm house kitchen diner in the south west of England.

Act 2: Scene 1: An upstairs room in Trellis and Vine.

Act 3: Scene 1: Double bedroom in Trellis and Vine.

Act 3: Scene 2: Same double bedroom in Trellis.

Act 4: Heron Tower – penthouse apartment.

INTERVAL

Act 5: Izabella's office above store in Brodham

Act 6: Trellis and Vine – bar area with adjoining reception.

Act 7: Double bedroom in Trellis and Vine.

Music break

Act 8: West Frampton post office.

Act 9: Motor Home in layby.

Act 10: Trellis and Vine

Other books by Sam Grant

Please check out these other publications by Sam Grant.
Follow blogs, poems and stories at
Samgrantpublications.wordpress.com
Sam Grant, Author – Facebook.

Atlantic Hijack (978-1-78222-291-0)
Action, mystery
Sea adventure in the South Atlantic
A secure orderly passage aboard a cargo liner is Ripped apart by a brutal terrorist attack. Author Sam Grant brings his professional seafaring experience to Bear in this thriller that sounds all too familiar from Our evening news bulletins. Apprentice Mike Peters is finding his feet amongst A cast of nautical characters as the Albany Princess Voyages to Montevideo. But the ship's personnel Are not all that they make themselves out to be as revealed during a rapidly unravelling hijack in the South Atlantic.

River Escape (978-1-68222-574-4)
Sequel to *Atlantic Hijack.*
Action, mystery,
Venezuela: An oil terminal in the River Orinoco, Venezuela. Following on from a military coup. Mike's pressured efforts to prepare the tanker For the load of boiler oil – compromised by a Refinery postponement.
An influential young woman, boards who starts calling, the shots? Hidden identity of a rescued yachtsman and two female companions further compromises the ship's safety ...

Dancing on the Beach (978-1-78222-431-0)
Romantic thriller
Phillip Norton obtains summer work as a deckchair attendant in Batcombe. Previously he works at a Bank in the City. Part of Phil's duties are to deliver Dairy cool boxes to the Sea View Hotel via the cliff railway. Soon he Is into a heady romance with the Receptionist. But with cruise liners anchored off Batcombe Bay the Sea View not Only hosts holidaymakers, but alsoHas connections with a more sinister trade...

Persuasion's Price (978-1-78222-687-1)
Mystery thriller
A Quiet market town in England is shattered by an explosive mix of gang rivalry and shady deals. A family is torn apart and, with the involvement of the secret services, events take an unexpected and sinister turn.

Galactic Mission (978-1 78222-512-6)
Science fiction
It is 2110. In an advanced technological world of holograms transmitted by mobile phones; food made by a Maxi Maker, drone trays, clones and automata concierges, QUADRANT is the world government. But the world is not at ease and relationships are put under strain. James Walters is a sales manager for an international conglomerate, based in the UK. One day he encounters Adriana – "The Empress Adriana" – from the Galactic Command Force …oh, and ruler of planet Earth and all Planets Force, with help from some Inspiring sources thwart planetary conflict.

Galactic Mission Part Two (978-1 -78222-773-1
Science fiction, sequel
In this classic sci-fi adventure, the main characters from Galactic Mission, including The Empress Adrian, are working to divert comets away from earth by firing a missile from Mars.
Adriana has decided to stay in human form, but seeks A closer relationship with James, who prefers Lara. He Backs away. Adriana is restricted in power, although Captain Dryson and Alfredo – two android machines – Carry out her instructions.
After the comets are directed away from earth, Galactic Force returns with Antar – XP200, and two new androids, to replace Adriana, on Mars. Adriana regains full power and a chosen group leaves for earth by space ship with the intention of gaining control over Quadrant, who are returning, now that earth has been saved?

Poetry and short story publications by Sam Grant

Poems with themed notes (978-1-78222-464-8)
Love Starved by Electronics is a sonnet selected for a 'Sonnets for Shakespeare' anthology.
In *Riding Through Time* ghostly horsemen appear to ride down the ages.
Captured into their Realm – a meeting with an Alien depicted in verse.
Eye of the Storm; The Time Makers Kingdom; Thankful Thoughts and *Spirit of Spring*. These are a few of the poems in this varied anthology.
Notes have been prepared and included by Sam Grant to give background information and set the poems in context.

Mists of Time (978-1-78222-708-3)
From epic poem to scary short story, *Mists of Time* entertains and enlightens. In the title poem, author Sam Grant takes us on A journey. Perhaps his journey, down a leafy
Lane to a farm in summer, off to sea and beyond.
Secret Cave is a short story informed by a Love of sail boat sailing, A reflection from the author's young life, before the author embarked On a career in the Merchant Service.
Part One – Poems both in traditional and modern form.
Dramatic, but also light-hearted topics explored.
Part Two – Short stories.
Individual cameo chapters.

Sam Grant, Author

    URL amazon.com/author/grantsam

    Samgrantpublications.wordpress.com

    Books are available from good book shops. Please give ISBN

www.ingramcontent.com/pod-product-compliance
Lightning Source LLC
Chambersburg PA
CBHW071410040426
42444CB00009B/2180